Common Core Mastery

Text-Based Writing Nonfiction

Grade 6

Contents

UNIT
1

Beyond the Canvas

Unit Focus

You are going to read a visual arts article about abstract expressionism.

As You Read:

Think about how Jackson Pollock and Mark Rothko were alike and different.

After You Read:

Use information from the article to write a compare-and-contrast essay about the painters' styles and paintings.

Lesson Checklist

Check off each task after you complete it.

☐ **Learn Vocabulary**

☐ **Read the Visual Arts Article:** *Beyond the Canvas*

☐ **Answer Questions About the Visual Arts Article**

☐ **Organize Information**

☐ **Write a Compare-and-Contrast Essay**

☐ **Evaluate Your Writing**

Learn Vocabulary

Read the word and its definition.
Then write the vocabulary word on the line.

1. **abstract**   not showing exactness or reality; unformed   *abstract*

2. **canvas**   cloth material that is stretched over a wood frame for paintings   *Canvas*

3. **complex**   difficult or complicated   *Complex*

4. **duplicate**   to make an exact copy of   *duplicate*

5. **easel**   a frame that is used to hold a canvas while one paints   *easel*

6. **fields**   large areas on a canvas that have been drawn on or painted   *fields*

7. **geometric**   relating to shapes such as straight lines, squares, or circles   *geometric*

8. **techniques**   the unique ways in which one works that are specific to the worker or artist   *techniques*

Beyond the Canvas

Abstract expressionism is a style of art that began in New York City in the mid-1900s, just after World War II. Abstract expressionism was a totally new idea in the art world that got its name because it's a combination of abstract art and expressionist art. The art is called abstract because it does not show something that is familiar to us, such as a person or a bowl of fruit.

Abstract expressionism tries to express emotions, feelings, or thoughts, and the usual techniques of painting are not used in this type of art. For example, paint can be applied to a canvas with tools other than brushes. Canvases are often so large that they are placed on the floor instead of on an easel. Jackson Pollock and Mark Rothko were two American artists who painted in the style of abstract expressionism. Their results, however, were very different. Pollock was known for his wild action paintings, and Rothko was known for his huge fields of color.

Action painting is about the process of making a painting. Jackson Pollock is known as the first action painter. Pollock would place a canvas on the floor instead of using an easel. He was known to use gallons of house paint straight from the cans and to apply the paint by using a stick. He poured, dripped, drizzled, and splashed paint onto each canvas. Pollock used a lot of energy and the weight of his body to paint.

Jackson Pollock

An example of an abstract painting showing action

He would paint from all four edges of a canvas. He wanted to be in the painting—to have the viewers of his paintings feel the action he used when he made them. Pollock was successful, because a viewer's eyes are always moving when looking at one of his works. There is never just one focus. Although Pollock's paintings may seem random, his drips were all carefully planned.

Color field painting is not about the process of making a painting—it's about showing feelings. Mark Rothko's paintings do not show people or objects. Instead, the artist used large fields of bold, solid colors on huge, flat canvases. The colors were layered and the shapes were geometric, though the edges were a bit blurred. Rothko believed that these shapes were the best way to show his deep feelings. He believed that the large

An example of color field painting

areas of color let viewers feel more than think. Rothko wanted viewers to stand so close to a painting of his that they would feel surrounded by the color—actually feel part of the painting itself. He also wanted viewers to feel the emotion he felt as he made the painting.

Although the paintings of Jackson Pollock and Mark Rothko might appear very simple, they are truly complex. Even though their techniques can be copied, no one can duplicate the artists' secret motives, moves, or emotions.

Rothko

Answer Questions

Read and answer each question.

1. Which of the following would be considered an abstract expressionist painting?

   Ⓐ one that shows no objects

   Ⓑ one that shows four family members

   Ⓒ one that shows bananas and oranges

2. Jackson Pollock put his canvases on the floor because he wanted ＿＿.

   Ⓐ to sit on the floor while painting

   Ⓑ viewers to see the painting from above

   Ⓒ to easily paint from all directions

3. Which of these did Mark Rothko use to show his deep feelings?

   Ⓐ squiggles and drips

   Ⓑ geometric shapes

   Ⓒ unusual canvases

4. Pollock most wanted viewers to feel his ＿＿.

   Ⓐ emotions

   Ⓑ desires

   Ⓒ actions

5. How do you think people felt about abstract expressionism when it first started? Why?

   I think people liked abstract expressionism
   because they enjoyed feeling like being in a painting,
   in the emotion.

6. Do you prefer Pollock's or Rothko's painting style? Why?

   I prefer Rothko's painting style because you
   can feel the emotion, also you can feel
   engaged in the painting

Organize Information

Read the art article again. Then write information in the Venn diagram that tells how the styles and paintings of Jackson Pollock and Mark Rothko are alike and different.

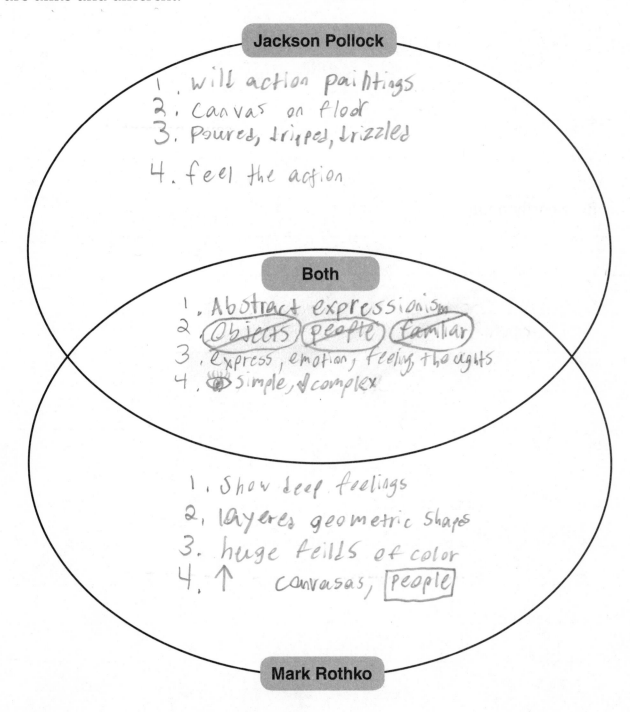

Jackson Pollock

1. will action paintings
2. Canvas on floor
3. Poured, dripped, drizzled
4. feel the action

Both

1. Abstract expressionism
2. Objects, people, familiar
3. express, emotion, feeling, thoughts
4. simple, & complex

Mark Rothko

1. Show deep feelings
2. layered geometric shapes
3. huge feilds of color
4. ↑ canvases, people

Compare and Contrast

Write a compare-and-contrast essay about **how Jackson Pollock and Mark Rothko were alike and different**. Describe their styles and paintings. Use information from your Venn diagram and the art article.

_____

Title

_____

_____

_____

_____

_____

_____

_____

_____

_____

_____

_____

Evaluate Your Writing

Read about the compare-and-contrast text structure. Then use your essay to complete the activity below.

A text that has a **compare-and-contrast** structure makes comparisons, or describes similarities between two or more things. It also contrasts, or describes how these things are different.

The reason for writing is clear.

My essay compared and contrasted:

_____

I used these compare-and-contrast signal words:

_____   _____   _____

I provided details that support the topic.

I included these detail sentences:

1. _____

2. _____

My paragraphs have a clear focus.

My opening sentence for the first paragraph is:

_____

My closing sentence for the first paragraph is:

_____

Finding Your Way

Unit Focus

You are going to read a science article about navigational tools.

As You Read:

Think about how compasses and maps are similar to and different from a GPS.

After You Read:

Use information from the article to write a compare-and-contrast essay about these tools.

Lesson Checklist

Check off each task after you complete it.

- [ ] **Learn Vocabulary**
- [ ] **Read the Science Article:** *Finding Your Way*
- [ ] **Answer Questions About the Science Article**
- [ ] **Organize Information**
- [ ] **Write a Compare-and-Contrast Essay**
- [ ] **Evaluate Your Writing**

Learn Vocabulary

Read the word and its definition.
Then write the vocabulary word on the line.

1. **approximate**   nearly correct or exact   _approximate_

2. **inexpensive**   not costing a lot of money; cheap   _inexpensive_

3. **navigation**   the science of locating the route between one place and another   _navigation_

4. **nomads**   people who regularly move instead of living in one place   _nomads_

5. **obsolete**   no longer useful or available   _obsolete_

6. **obstacles**   physical objects in the way of one's path   _obstacles_

7. **revolutionized**   made vastly different; changed completely in a beneficial way   _revolutionized_

8. **satellites**   machines that orbit Earth   _satellites_

9. **sea currents**   strong movements of water in the world's oceans   _sea currents_

Finding Your Way

Chances are the car your family drives or the cellphone you use has a GPS, or Global Positioning System. A GPS is a navigational tool that uses advanced technology to help people find locations. There are many uses for a GPS, and most people agree that it is one of the best navigational tools available today.

A GPS is made up of three parts. First, there is a group of satellites that circle Earth. Next, there are control stations that monitor the satellites and make sure they are working correctly. Finally, there are GPS receivers that receive radio signals from the satellites. The satellites are owned by the United States Department of Defense, but they can be used by anyone who has a receiver.

SATELLITES IN SPACE

CONTROL STATIONS

GPS RECEIVERS

For a GPS to work, there has to be a clear path of communication between the receiver and some of the satellites.

To use a GPS, the user turns on the machine. The receiver then searches for signals from the various satellites, and the information is sent to the user's machine.

A GPS can tell you where you are, where you are going, the best way to get there, and the approximate time you will arrive, depending on your route and speed.

Because a GPS shows you maps, routes, and specific locations, some people wonder how they ever got anywhere without this high-tech tool. Humans have been navigating the land and water on Earth for thousands of years. The first explorers and sailors used the most basic techniques to navigate their walking routes or ships and to know their own locations. They relied on sight, winds, sea currents, and the positions of the sun and stars in the sky. The sky was their map.

These basic techniques were useful, but accurate, long-term exploration of our planet required more advanced tools. The compass revolutionized navigation. A compass allowed sailors or nomads to continue moving in a specific direction when bad weather made the sun and the stars difficult to see. Eventually, the compass led to the development of maps, which became more and more accurate. Over time, the tools used for navigation expanded. Today, some people say that

A compass is a small tool that shows directions relative to Earth's surface.

a GPS makes older navigational tools outdated and useless. Others believe that compasses and maps are as valuable as ever. There are valid arguments for both.

Compasses and maps can be considered better than a GPS because they don't need batteries or radio signals to work. They are inexpensive compared to a GPS and can easily be stored or placed on a table for study. GPS machines may not always work in certain locations because their radio signals may be blocked by obstacles such as buildings or wooded areas. On the other hand, a GPS can be considered better than compasses and maps because it may be more accurate and easier to use. It will quickly tell you how much distance you've covered and how much farther you have to go. It also has multiple kinds of maps that are instantly available to users. A GPS can save time and is useful in emergency situations, such as tracking a lost child or pet.

Some people believe that maps and compasses will be obsolete in the future, while others believe that they will be around as long as humans have the need to travel. Either way, both tools certainly have advantages and disadvantages. Which tool will you use?

Answer Questions

Read and answer each question.

1. Which of the following does a GPS need in order to function properly?

   Ⓐ a table on which to study it

   Ⓑ exposure to sea currents

   Ⓒ a clear path to satellites

2. The function of a compass is to show _____.

   Ⓐ directions

   Ⓑ landmasses

   Ⓒ waterways

3. Some people prefer compasses and maps because they do not require _____.

   Ⓐ reading

   Ⓑ understanding directions

   Ⓒ batteries

4. A GPS would work better than a standard map for _____.

   Ⓐ seeing the shapes of various countries

   Ⓑ locating a lost child at a shopping center

   Ⓒ finding your route through an underground cave

5. How did early explorers use the sun and the stars to travel? Explain.

   They track the north star or look at the sun
   to see which direction they should go in.

6. The article ends with a question. What is your answer? Why?

   I use a GPS because it is available
   everywhere, easy to use, and can find
   lost people and animals.

Organize Information

Read the science article again. Then write information in the Venn diagram that tells how compasses and maps are similar to and different from a GPS.

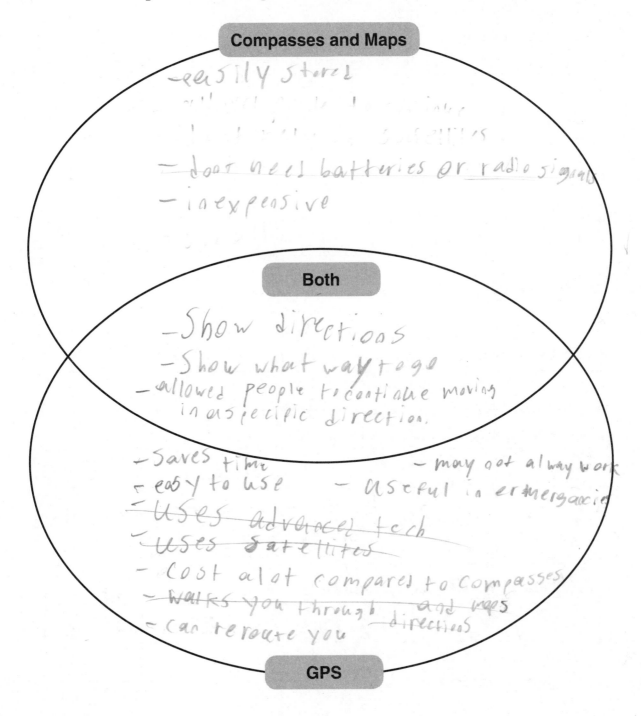

Compasses and Maps

- easily stored
- *(illegible)* ... satellites
- doot need batteries or radio signals
- inexpensive

Both

- Show directions
- Show what way to go
- allowed people to continue moving in a specific direction.

GPS

- Saves time
- easy to use
- Uses advanced tech
- Uses satellites
- Cost alot compared to compasses
- walks you through directions and maps
- can reroute you
- may not always work
- useful in emergencies

Compare and Contrast

Write a compare-and-contrast essay about **how compasses and maps are similar to and different from a GPS**. Use information from your Venn diagram and the science article.

Travel Options
_____
Title

If your planning a trip to Somwhere nowadays
One of the first things you'll do is pull out
your phone and check the GPS. The GPS will
Show you how long to get there along with
step-by-step directions. A GPS uses advanced
technology, batteries, and satellites to operate.
Before GPS was around people used maps
and compases. They're not used as much anymore
but they still have value in them because they
dont rely on batteries and radio signals
as much as a GPS. They also are inexpensive
compared to a GPS. A GPS are

A GPS or compass and map will each
lead you to your destination. Both options will
lead you in one direction. GPS' and compass
and map both have advantages and disadvantages. I
believe it would be best to carry both travel options just in case
one doesnt work.

Evaluate Your Writing

Read about the compare-and-contrast text structure. Then use your essay to complete the activity below.

> A text that has a **compare-and-contrast** structure makes comparisons, or describes similarities between two or more things. It also contrasts, or describes how these things are different.

The reason for writing is clear.

My essay compared and contrasted:

_____

I used these compare-and-contrast signal words:

_____   _____   _____

I provided details that support the topic.

I included these detail sentences:

1. _____

2. _____

My paragraphs have a clear focus.

My opening sentence for the first paragraph is:

_____

My closing sentence for the first paragraph is:

_____

UNIT
3

The Benefits of Laughter

Unit Focus

You are going to read a health article about laughter.

As You Read:

Think about the mental and physical benefits of laughter.

After You Read:

Use information from the article to write a cause-and-effect essay about the benefits of laughter.

Lesson Checklist

Check off each task after you complete it.

- [ ] **Learn Vocabulary**

- [ ] **Read the Health Article:**
  The Benefits of Laughter

- [ ] **Answer Questions About the Health Article**

- [ ] **Organize Information**

- [ ] **Write a Cause-and-Effect Essay**

- [ ] **Evaluate Your Writing**

Learn Vocabulary

Read the word and its definition.
Then write the vocabulary word on the line.

1. **blood pressure**   the pressure that is put on the blood vessels in one's body when the heart beats   _____

2. **contort**   to move in an odd or unnatural way   _____

3. **defuse**   to make less dangerous or uncomfortable   _____

4. **endorphins**   natural chemicals in the brain that make humans feel good or happy   _____

5. **immunity**   the body's ability to resist disease   _____

6. **larynx**   the part of the upper throat that allows humans to speak or make sounds   _____

7. **psychological**   relating to the mind or thoughts   _____

8. **resilience**   the ability to stay strong or brave during hard times   _____

The Benefits of Laughter

What makes you laugh? Does a funny joke crack you up? Do you burst out giggling when you're nervous? You know that you laugh because something is funny, but did you know that laughing can be good for your health? There are many researchers and scientists who study laughter and can confirm that the health benefits are real.

Laughter is good for our physical and psychological well-being, but there are still a lot of questions about why humans laugh. It might seem that we laugh to make ourselves feel good, but many researchers say that the main purpose for human laughter is to bring people together. They say that by connecting with each other through laughter, both our physical health and psychological health improve. The health benefits are the positive side effects.

The act of laughing can cause a number of things to happen to our brains and bodies. When we laugh, our brains release endorphins. Endorphins make us better able to handle stressful situations or to feel relaxed in group settings. By sharing laughter with others, we feel that we are part of the group—that we belong.

Depending on how we are laughing, there are some physical changes we go through as well. We make sounds, such as hiccuping or coughing noises. We might even laugh so hard that we cry. Our faces change—we use about 15 of our face muscles when we laugh. Our bodies move, twist, or contort. The larynx might half close, making it hard for us to catch our breath or to speak because air can't get into and out of the body as well as it normally can.

Despite the odd things that happen to our bodies as we laugh, scientific studies have shown that laughter can have many positive effects on health. One of those effects is providing a good workout. Laughter works stomach, facial, leg, and back muscles. Studies show that laughing 100 times has the same effect as being on a rowing machine for 10 minutes or an exercise bike for 15 minutes.

HUMAN LAUGHTER		
Physical Health Benefits	**Mental Health Benefits**	**Social Benefits**
Boosts immunity	Adds joy and zest to life	Strengthens relationships
Reduces the effects of stress	Improves memory and learning	Builds confidence
Decreases pain	Relieves stress	Enhances teamwork
Relaxes muscles	Improves mood	Helps defuse conflict
Lowers blood pressure	Enhances resilience	Promotes group bonding

Even if nothing seems funny to you right now, you can create opportunities to laugh in the near future. Try some of these activities, and you'll be laughing in no time:

- Watch a funny movie or TV show.
- Read cartoons or comics.
- Share a good joke or a funny story.
- Check out a book from the humor section at the library.
- Play with a pet.
- Do something silly.
- Plan a fun outing with friends.

Now that you've read about the health benefits of laughter and activities that can make you laugh, you are better prepared to improve your health and the health of those around you with a simple giggle.

Answer Questions

Read and answer each question.

1. Many researchers believe that humans laugh in order to ____.
   - Ⓐ make themselves feel better
   - Ⓑ bond with other humans
   - Ⓒ exercise their stomachs

2. When endorphins are released, a person's ____ is lowered.
   - Ⓐ stress level
   - Ⓑ ability to laugh
   - Ⓒ immune system

3. Which of the following is a social benefit of laughter?
   - Ⓐ enhanced teamwork
   - Ⓑ improved memory
   - Ⓒ fewer infections

4. Laughter is good for your body's overall health because it ____.
   - Ⓐ moves your facial muscles
   - Ⓑ half closes your larynx
   - Ⓒ is a form of physical exercise

5. Why do you think humans enjoy being "part of the group"?

   _____

   _____

6. Describe the last time you laughed really hard. What made you laugh and why?

   _____

   _____

Organize Information

Read the health article again. Then write information in the graphic organizer that tells the causes and effects of laughter.

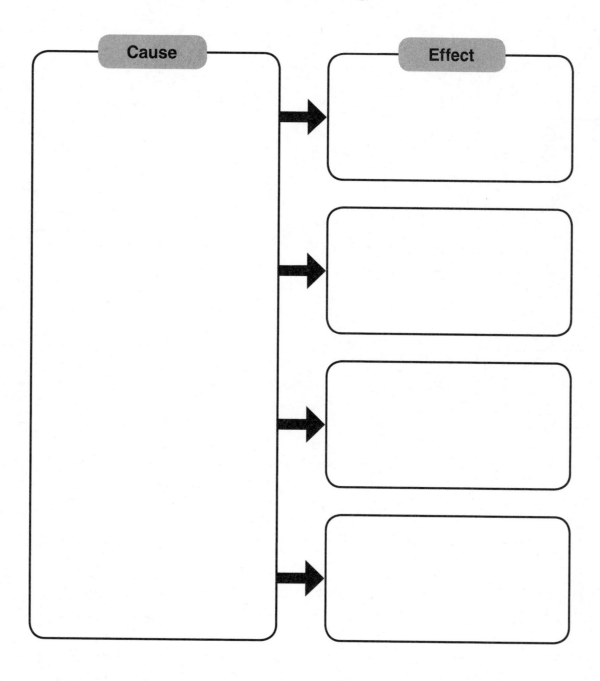

Cause

Effect

Cause and Effect

Write a cause-and-effect essay about **the benefits of laughter**. Use information from your graphic organizer and the health article.

_____
Title

_____

_____

_____

_____

_____

_____

_____

_____

_____

_____

_____

_____

_____

_____

_____

_____

Evaluate Your Writing

Read about the cause-and-effect text structure. Then use your essay to complete the activity below.

> A text that has a **cause-and-effect** structure tells what happens (effect) and why it happens (cause). It also tells if a cause has multiple effects.

The reason for writing is clear.

My essay described the cause-and-effect relationship(s) between: _____

_____

I used these cause-and-effect signal words:

_____   _____   _____

I provided details that support the topic.

I included these detail sentences:

   1. _____

   2. _____

My paragraphs have a clear focus.

My first paragraph explains that _____

caused (or causes) _____

My last paragraph summarizes the cause-and-effect relationship(s) with this sentence:

_____

UNIT
4

Motion Sickness

Unit Focus

You are going to read a health article about motion sickness.

As You Read:

Think about the cause and multiple effects of this illness.

After You Read:

Use information from the article to write a cause-and-effect essay about motion sickness.

Lesson Checklist

Check off each task after you complete it.

- [ ] Learn Vocabulary
- [ ] Read the Health Article: *Motion Sickness*
- [ ] Answer Questions About the Health Article
- [ ] Organize Information
- [ ] Write a Cause-and-Effect Essay
- [ ] Evaluate Your Writing

Learn Vocabulary

Read the word and its definition.
Then write the vocabulary word on the line.

1. **coincide**   to agree or match up with;
                        to happen at the same time   _____

2. **confirmed**   proven to be factual or correct   _____

3. **conjunction**   together or at the same time   _____

4. **fatigue**   tiredness or exhaustion   _____

5. **immobile**   being still or not moving   _____

6. **prevention**   the act of stopping an action
                        from happening in advance   _____

7. **static**   motionless   _____

8. **term**   a scientific or technical word
                        that defines a topic or condition   _____

Motion Sickness

If you have ever had motion sickness, you are not alone. Motion sickness is the term used for the sick feeling some people can get when they are riding in a vehicle. The vehicle can be a car, bus, plane, train, or boat. People who travel are not the only ones who can be affected by this disorder. Even simple, fun activities can trigger the illness. Amusement park rides, watching movies, and playing video games can all lead to motion sickness. It can happen to anyone—children, adults, even highly-trained people with special jobs. For example, astronauts can get spacesick, sailors can get seasick, and even champion race car drivers have been known to get carsick.

Although experts have not confirmed the exact causes of motion sickness, the people who are sick know one thing for sure: they *don't* feel good. The symptoms of motion sickness can include dizziness, fatigue, upset stomach, headache, sweating, and vomiting. Curvy roads, bumpy airplane rides, rolling waves, and roller coaster loops can all lead to motion sickness. But why do these conditions affect some more than others?

Your eyes and inner ears work in conjunction to let your brain know that you're moving or staying still. They also help confirm that you're balanced as you move. The eyes and inner ears, as well as other body parts such as muscles, send signals to the brain that most times agree. They allow you to feel steady and firmly balanced. But if the inner ears sense motion and the eyes do not, the signals that go to the brain do not coincide. This can cause visual motion sickness, which is the most common type.

Imagine that you are on a boat, but you're sitting down below the deck in a room that has no windows. Your eyes tell you that you're immobile. Your inner ears, however, let you know that you are rocking back and forth or traveling forward along the water. In that instant, your senses do not agree. Each part of the body sends a different signal to the brain. The result can be motion sickness. As another example, imagine that you're riding in a car while reading a book. Your eyes are looking at a page, so they tell your brain that the page is static. In addition, your muscles tell your brain that you are sitting still. At the same time, as the car moves along, your inner ears tell your brain that you are moving. Your brain gets confused, and you can feel sick.

According to the Centers for Disease Control and Prevention (CDC), where you sit in a vehicle can make a big difference. Try to choose a seat that will have the least amount of motion. For example, sitting in the front seat of a car might be helpful, and wing seats in a plane might give you a smoother ride. The CDC also recommends looking out into the distance instead of trying to read or looking at something within the vehicle. This can help your body and brain take in similar information.

Additional tips include:
- If you are on a long car trip, make frequent stops along the way and walk around.
- If possible, open a window to breathe fresh air.
- Listen to the radio, sing, or talk.
- Place a cool cloth on your forehead.
- Try to keep your head still.

Motion sickness can be difficult to deal with, but if you prepare your mind and body, you can lessen the effects of motion.

Answer Questions

Read and answer each question.

1. Motion sickness occurs when your eyes and your ___ send conflicting messages to your brain.

   Ⓐ stomach

   Ⓑ inner ears

   Ⓒ legs

2. You can feel motion sickness if you are lacking a sense of ___.

   Ⓐ hearing

   Ⓑ balance

   Ⓒ strength

3. Which of the following is least likely to cause motion sickness?

   Ⓐ walking on a trail

   Ⓑ riding on a bus

   Ⓒ flying in an airplane

4. Which of these could help if you have motion sickness?

   Ⓐ reading a book

   Ⓑ playing a video game

   Ⓒ breathing some fresh air

5. What might cause an astronaut to get spacesick?

   _____

   _____

6. Do you think closing your eyes might help you if you have motion sickness? Why or why not?

   _____

   _____

Organize Information

Read the health article again. Then write information in the graphic organizer that tells the cause and effects of motion sickness.

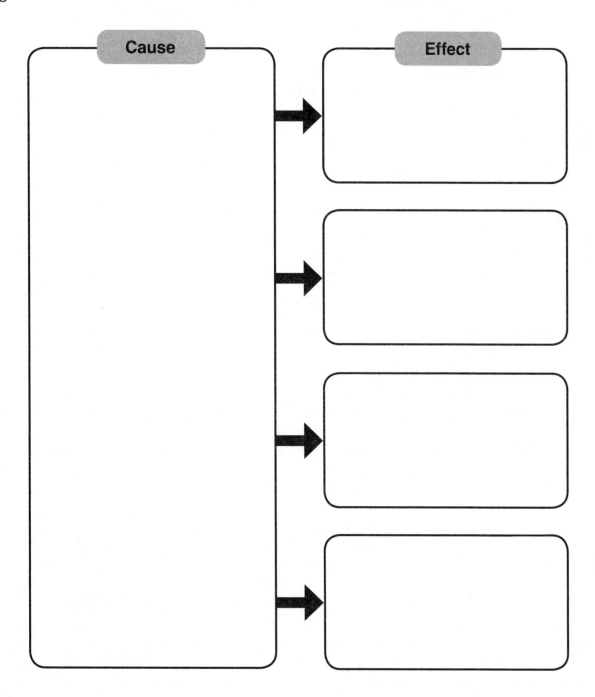

Cause and Effect

Write a cause-and-effect essay that tells **what happens when people get motion sickness and why**. Use information from your graphic organizer and the health article.

_____

Title

_____

_____

_____

_____

_____

_____

_____

_____

_____

_____

_____

_____

Evaluate Your Writing

Read about the cause-and-effect text structure. Then use your essay to complete the activity below.

> A text that has a **cause-and-effect** structure tells what happens (effect) and why it happens (cause). It also tells if a cause has multiple effects.

The reason for writing is clear.

My essay described the cause-and-effect relationship(s) between: _____

_____

I used these cause-and-effect signal words:

_____   _____   _____

I provided details that support the topic.

I included these detail sentences:

1. _____

2. _____

My paragraphs have a clear focus.

My first paragraph explains that _____

caused (or causes) _____

My last paragraph summarizes the cause-and-effect relationship(s) with this sentence:

_____

Jennifer Rodriguez

Unit Focus

You are going to read a biography about Jennifer Rodriguez.

As You Read:

Think about how the different events in her life helped her to become successful in many ways.

After You Read:

Use information from the biography to write a cause-and-effect essay about Jennifer Rodriguez's success.

Lesson Checklist

Check off each task after you complete it.

- [ ] Learn Vocabulary

- [ ] Read the Biography: *Jennifer Rodriguez*

- [ ] Answer Questions About the Biography

- [ ] Organize Information

- [ ] Write a Cause-and-Effect Essay

- [ ] Evaluate Your Writing

Learn Vocabulary

Read the word and its definition.
Then write the vocabulary word on the line.

1. **exercise physiology**   the study of how human bodies change when they are exposed to a lot of exercise

   _____

2. **figure skating**   a sport in which a person performs jumps, spins, and dance movements while on ice skates or wheeled skates

   _____

3. **influence**   the power of a person to affect someone in a positive or negative way

   _____

4. **persistence**   the act of trying an action over and over again, even if one fails

   _____

5. **pertained**   related to; had to do with

   _____

6. **qualify**   to be able to participate in an event or on a team as a result of physical training

   _____

7. **retire**   to stop working

   _____

8. **rigorous**   extremely difficult or demanding

   _____

Jennifer Rodriguez

Jennifer Rodriguez was born in 1976 in Miami, Florida. As a child, Rodriguez discovered a talent for roller-skating. By the age of four, she was taking lessons. When she was five years old, she competed in figure roller-skating and roller speed skating. She continued to compete in figure roller-skating and inline speed roller-skating for many years. In 1994, Rodriguez became the only woman to win medals in both figure roller-skating and roller racing events. Also in 1994, she graduated from high school and then attended Florida International University.

In 1996, Rodriguez switched to the ice sport of speed skating and wanted to qualify for the United States Winter Olympics team. She competed in the 1998 games in Nagano, Japan. Although she'd only been competing in speed skating for about a year, she finished in fourth place. Some people had predicted that she wouldn't finish in the top ten, but because of her hard work, dedication, and training, Rodriguez proved them all wrong. In the 2002 games in Salt Lake City, Utah, Rodriguez was the first American woman to earn a spot in all five distance events— 500, 1,000, 1,500, 3,000, and 5,000 meters. She won two bronze medals, which made her the first Cuban American to compete in and win a medal at the Winter Olympics.

Although Rodriguez made the 2006 Olympic team, she did not win a medal that year in Turin, Italy. In 2009, she decided to retire. Also during that year, she faced the challenge of losing her mother, who passed away from cancer. According to Rodriguez, it was the worst year of her life. Her mother had been a huge influence and had taught her many lessons that pertained to sports and life in general. From the time Rodriguez started roller-skating lessons, her mother had taught her the importance of persistence. Rodriguez once told an interviewer that her mom "was always about giving it more than 110 percent." She believes that the strength and determination she has always had comes straight from her mom.

Text-Based Writing: Nonfiction • EMC 6446 • © Evan-Moor Corp.

In 2010, Rodriguez decided to return to major competition one last time and compete at the Winter Olympics in Vancouver, Canada. She was determined to have fun and enjoy herself. In the past, Rodriguez had focused only on skating, and the rigorous training took over her entire experience at the games. As an older, mature athlete, she wanted to have balance in 2010. She felt no pressure and, even though she didn't win a medal that year, she had a great time.

In May of 2013, Rodriguez graduated from the University of Miami with a degree in exercise physiology. She was very proud of her academic accomplishment. According to Rodriguez, studying never came as easy to her as skating had. She had participated in sports her whole life—and she *knew* she was good at them. For Rodriguez, earning a college degree was harder and, in some ways, more rewarding than winning any medal.

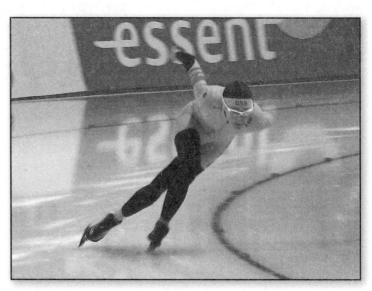

Jennifer Rodriquez speed skating

Jennifer Rodriguez's Medals in Speed Skating		
Medal Type	**Olympic Games**	**Race**
Bronze	2002; Salt Lake City, Utah	1,000 meters
Bronze	2002; Salt Lake City, Utah	1,500 meters
Medal Type	**World Championships**	**Race**
Gold	2005; Salt Lake City, Utah	Sprint
Silver	2003; Berlin, Germany	1,000 meters
Bronze	2005; Inzell, Germany	1,500 meters
Bronze	2004; Seoul, South Korea	1,500 meters
Bronze	2004; Nagano, Japan	Sprint
Bronze	2003; Berlin, Germany	1,500 meters

Answer Questions

Read and answer each question.

1. The first sport Jennifer Rodriguez participated in was ____.

   Ⓐ ice speed skating

   Ⓑ inline speed roller-skating

   Ⓒ figure roller-skating

2. In what year did Rodriguez participate in her first Winter Olympics?

   Ⓐ 1994

   Ⓑ 1996

   Ⓒ 1998

3. Rodriguez was the first American woman to compete ____.

   Ⓐ in five speed-skating distance events

   Ⓑ to win a gold medal

   Ⓒ in the Winter Olympics

4. In which race did Rodriguez win her only gold medal?

   Ⓐ the 2002 U.S. Winter Olympics 1,500 meters

   Ⓑ the 2004 Japan World Championships sprint

   Ⓒ the 2005 Utah World Championships sprint

5. Which ice speed-skating race was the best kind for Rodriguez to compete in? How do you know?

   _____

   _____

6. In your own words, explain why Rodriguez had such a nice time at the 2010 Winter Olympics.

   _____

   _____

Organize Information

Read the biography again. Then write information in the graphic organizer that lists causes and effects in Jennifer Rodriguez's life that led to her success.

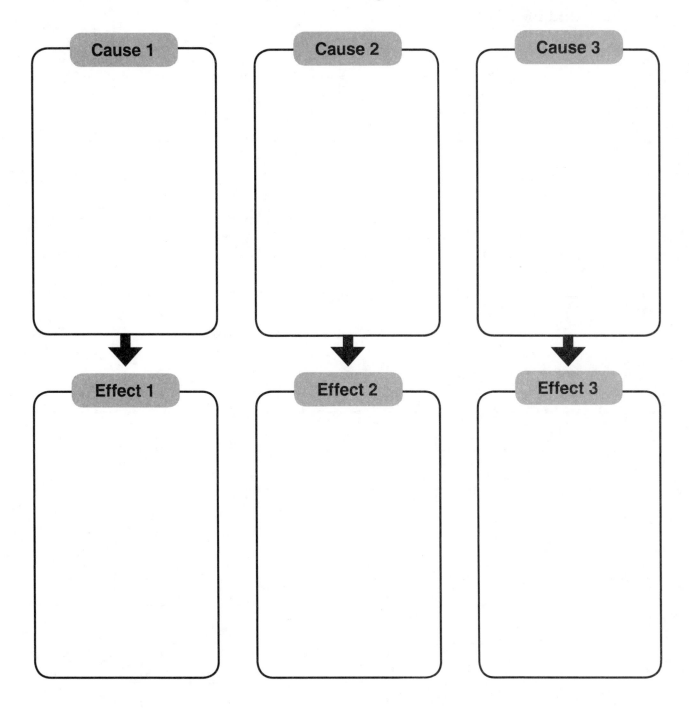

Cause 1

Cause 2

Cause 3

Effect 1

Effect 2

Effect 3

Cause and Effect

Write a cause-and-effect essay about **how Jennifer Rodriguez became successful in sports and in life**. Use information from your graphic organizer and the biography.

_____

Title

_____

_____

_____

_____

_____

_____

_____

_____

_____

_____

_____

Evaluate Your Writing

Read about the cause-and-effect text structure. Then use your essay to complete the activity below.

> A text that has a **cause-and-effect** structure tells what happens (effect) and why it happens (cause). It also tells if a cause has multiple effects.

The reason for writing is clear.

My essay described the cause-and-effect relationship(s) between: _____

_____

I used these cause-and-effect signal words:

_____   _____   _____

I provided details that support the topic.

I included these detail sentences:

   1. _____

   2. _____

My paragraphs have a clear focus.

My first paragraph explains that _____

caused (or causes) _____

My last paragraph summarizes the cause-and-effect relationship(s) with this sentence:

_____

Fancy Fliers

Unit Focus

You are going to read a science article about hummingbirds.

As You Read:

Think about how these birds work within their habitats to stay alive.

After You Read:

Use information from the article to write an explanatory essay about how hummingbirds work to survive.

Lesson Checklist

Check off each task after you complete it.

- [ ] **Learn Vocabulary**
- [ ] **Read the Science Article:** *Fancy Fliers*
- [ ] **Answer Questions About the Science Article**
- [ ] **Organize Information**
- [ ] **Write an Explanatory Essay**
- [ ] **Evaluate Your Writing**

Learn Vocabulary

Read the word and its definition.
Then write the vocabulary word on the line.

1. **evolve**   to change or develop in a new
                         and beneficial way   _____

2. **habitat**   natural surroundings in which
                         an animal, bird, or insect lives   _____

3. **nectar**   a sweet liquid found inside
                         flowers   _____

4. **observe**   to watch or study carefully   _____

5. **pistils**   the female reproductive parts
                         of flowers (the seeds develop
                         here)   _____

6. **stamens**   the male reproductive parts
                         of flowers (the pollen is
                         produced here)   _____

7. **territorial**   defensive or protective of one's
                         space or area   _____

8. **traits**   characteristics   _____

Fancy Fliers

Did you know that there are over 300 species of hummingbirds? Most of these species live in the tropical forests of Central and South America. If you have seen a hummingbird in your yard, it is likely one of about 20 species that live in North America. The hummingbirds here like to visit yards with flowers or feeders that

A hummingbird drinking nectar

are filled with their favorite food—nectar. When hummingbirds are around a food source, you might be able to observe the unusual ways they are able to move. They dash, dart, zip, and flip upside down. They even fly backwards and can float in midair. These hummingbirds are not playing—they're working to find and eat food.

Hummingbirds might look like cute little creatures, but they're very aggressive when they need to find food. In tropical forests, feeders are not provided by humans. Hummingbirds face many challenges in nature, but they have several adaptations to make their job easier. Adaptations are body parts, body coverings, or behaviors that help an animal survive in its habitat. The behaviors of hummingbirds might seem complex, but their mission is simple. They need to continuously fly to eat and eat to fly.

For hummingbirds, finding food is a daily job, and it takes a lot of energy. After all, they have to visit hundreds of flowers a day in order to get enough of the sugary nectar they need. The problem is that they can only store enough food in their bodies to survive overnight. In addition to having to find food, hummingbirds also have to guard their food sources. They are very territorial and they work hard to guard their favorite flower patches. If any other bird or even a bee or a butterfly tries to take its food, a hummingbird will attack.

While all hummingbirds have the same basic traits, there are some species of hummingbirds that are truly unique. The sword-billed hummingbird of South Africa is one example. The sword-bill is one of the largest hummingbird species, not because of its body size but because of the amazing length of its bill. This bird's bill can be up to 4 inches long, which is about 3 inches longer than its body! The bird's tongue is also

A sword-billed hummingbird

very long. The bill and tongue are adapted, or designed, to get nectar from flowers that have long corollas. Corollas are the parts of the flowers that include the petals and hold the stamens and pistils.

Because of their unique bills and tongues, the sword-billed hummingbirds can drink nectar from a passionflower. In fact, sword-bills are the only birds that can reach the nectar deep inside these flowers. These two species have a very close connection. The two of them evolve together, so they affect each other's ability to grow and survive. When the sword-bill feeds from the flower, its pollen sticks to the bird. When the bird flies away, it carries the pollen to a new passionflower, which then helps that plant to reproduce. However, experts say that by feeding on just one type of flower, the sword-bill could become at risk of extinction. In order to thrive, the sword-bill may need to adapt in a brand-new way in the future.

Answer Questions

Read and answer each question.

1. In tropical forests, hummingbirds cannot eat from ____.

   Ⓐ passionflowers

   Ⓑ nectar feeders

   Ⓒ flowers

2. How many flowers does a typical hummingbird need to visit each day?

   Ⓐ 10 to 20

   Ⓑ 2 to 50

   Ⓒ 200 or more

3. The sword-billed hummingbird uses its long bill to get nectar from a passionflower's ____.

   Ⓐ pollen

   Ⓑ petals

   Ⓒ corolla

4. Flowers rely on hummingbirds to help the flowers ____.

   Ⓐ transport pollen

   Ⓑ stay protected from other birds

   Ⓒ produce nectar

5. What might happen if all the passionflowers died off?

   _____

   _____

6. What might happen if you tried to remove a hummingbird's sources of food? Why?

   _____

   _____

Organize Information

Read the science article again. Then write information in the graphic organizer that explains how hummingbirds work to stay alive.

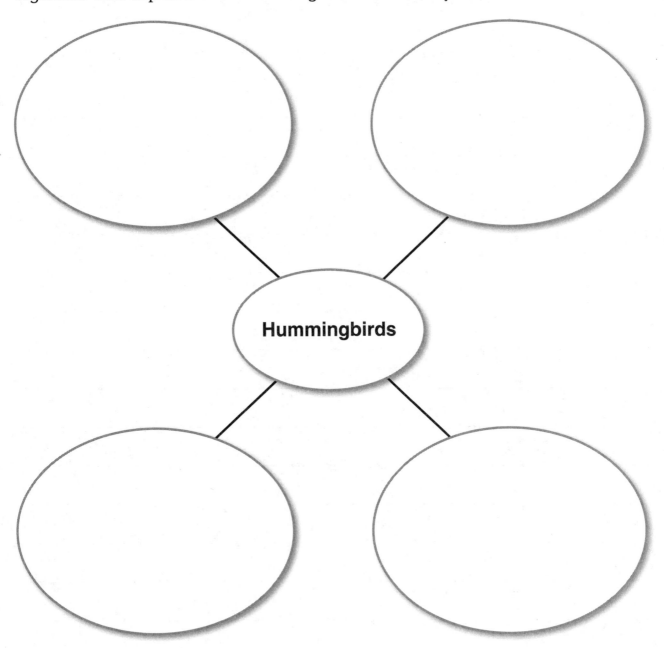

Hummingbirds

Explain

Write an explanatory essay about **how hummingbirds work to survive**.
Use information from your graphic organizer and the science article.

_____

Title

_____

_____

_____

_____

_____

_____

_____

_____

_____

_____

_____

Evaluate Your Writing

Read about the explanatory text structure. Then use your essay to complete the activity below.

A text that has an **explanatory** structure provides the answers to the following questions: *Why? Where?* or *How?* It also provides detailed information about the topic.

The reason for writing is clear.

My essay explained:

_____

I introduced the subject in this topic sentence:

_____

I provided details that support the topic.

I included these detail sentences:

1. _____

2. _____

My paragraphs have a clear focus.

My first paragraph explains that:

_____

My last paragraph includes this conclusion sentence:

_____

UNIT
7

The United Nations

Unit Focus

You are going to read a social studies article about the United Nations.

As You Read:

Think about why the United Nations was formed and how it works.

After You Read:

Use information from the article to write an explanatory essay about why the United Nations is so important to the world.

Lesson Checklist

Check off each task after you complete it.

☐ **Learn Vocabulary**

☐ **Read the Social Studies Article:** *The United Nations*

☐ **Answer Questions About the Social Studies Article**

☐ **Organize Information**

☐ **Write an Explanatory Essay**

☐ **Evaluate Your Writing**

Learn Vocabulary

Read the word and its definition.
Then write the vocabulary word on the line.

1. **agencies**   small groups within a governing group or government that help with specific tasks   _____

2. **alliance**   a beneficial and helpful relationship between two or more groups   _____

3. **civilians**   people who are not part of the military or law enforcement   _____

4. **contract**   a written agreement signed by two or more parties   _____

5. **human rights**   the basic freedoms that every person deserves   _____

6. **illiteracy**   the inability to read or write   _____

7. **principles**   rules or laws   _____

8. **values**   ideas that people believe in or feel are very important   _____

The United Nations

The United Nations, or UN, is an international organization comprised of different countries that are in an alliance. The main purpose of the UN is to support peace and security among the nations of the world and to prevent war. The organization is guided

by certain principles and values that emphasize equality and cooperation among all member countries. It also works to find peaceful solutions to any disagreements between nations. The principles are described in the Charter of the United Nations. The Charter is a contract that requires member nations to uphold these principles.

Among other things, the member countries agree to:

- maintain international peace and security
- develop friendly relations among nations
- cooperate in solving international problems and in promoting respect for human rights
- be a center for harmonizing the actions of nations

The United Nations was formed in 1945 after World War II, which was one of our world's most devastating wars. An estimated 60 million people died, 40 million of whom were civilians. World War II disrupted many cities and countries, causing people to leave their homes and move to new lands. Many families were separated, and there were times of extreme poverty and hunger.

After World War II, several countries, including the United States, China, Great Britain, the Soviet Union, and France, called for cooperation among nations. They wanted to work together to keep another worldwide war from erupting in the future. Eventually, a total of 51 countries came together to talk about how to achieve their goals. That was the beginning of the United Nations.

Today, 193 countries are members of the UN. UN headquarters are located in New York City. The main job of the UN is still to uphold peace and security for all of its member countries. In fact, the United Nations' emblem is a map of the world surrounded by a wreath of olive branches. The olive branch is a symbol of peace.

In addition to supporting peace, the UN also exists to serve people in need, whether they are affected by poverty, hunger, disease, illiteracy, or discrimination. A variety of special programs and agencies exist to make sure the rights of people from all walks of life are upheld.

The United Nations' Services	
Provides food to 90 million people in 75 countries	Combats climate change; works with 140 nations to prevent harmful mercury emissions
Assists over 34 million refugees and people fleeing war, famine, or persecution	Vaccinates 58% of the world's children, saving 2.5 million lives a year
Keeps the peace with 120,000 peacekeepers in 16 operations on 4 continents	Uses diplomacy to prevent conflict; assists some 50 countries a year with elections
Protects and promotes human rights on-site and through 80 treaties/declarations	Fights poverty, helping 370 million rural poor achieve better lives in the last 30 years
Mobilizes $12.5 billion in humanitarian aid to help people affected by emergencies	Promotes maternal health, saving the lives of 30 million women a year

Answer Questions

Read and answer each question.

1. The primary goal of the United Nations is to _____.

    Ⓐ uphold the laws of the individual member countries

    Ⓑ maintain peace and cooperation between countries

    Ⓒ provide education for literacy programs

2. The United Nations was formed after World War II because _____.

    Ⓐ 51 countries worked together to end that war

    Ⓑ many countries were suffering from disease and discrimination

    Ⓒ some countries wanted to work together to prevent future wars

3. How many people does the United Nations provide food for?

    Ⓐ 2.5 million

    Ⓑ 90 million

    Ⓒ 140 million

4. What do the olive branches on the United Nations' emblem symbolize?

    Ⓐ peace

    Ⓑ human rights

    Ⓒ climate change

5. Why might some countries not want to join the United Nations?

    _____

    _____

    _____

6. Is another worldwide war more likely or less likely to happen today? Why?

    _____

    _____

Organize Information

Read the social studies article again. Then write information in the graphic organizer that explains why the United Nations is so important to the world.

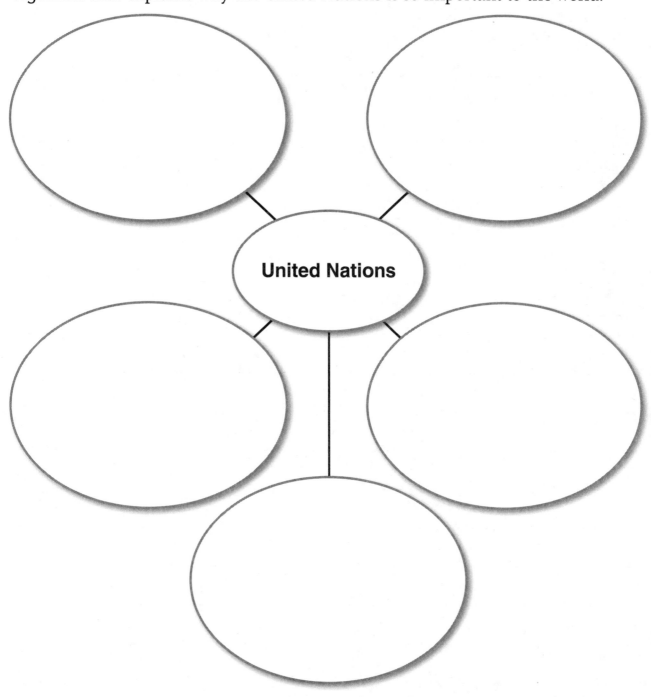

United Nations

Explain

Write an explanatory essay about **why the United Nations is so important to the world**. Use information from your graphic organizer and the social studies article.

_____
Title

_____

_____

_____

_____

_____

_____

_____

_____

_____

_____

_____

_____

_____

Evaluate Your Writing

Read about the explanatory text structure. Then use your essay to complete the activity below.

A text that has an **explanatory** structure provides the answers to the following questions: *Why? Where?* or *How?* It also provides detailed information about the topic.

The reason for writing is clear.

My essay explained:

_____

I introduced the subject in this topic sentence:

_____

I provided details that support the topic.

I included these detail sentences:

1. _____

2. _____

My paragraphs have a clear focus.

My first paragraph explains that:

_____

My last paragraph includes this conclusion sentence:

_____

Koa Halpern

Unit Focus

You are going to read a biography about Koa Halpern.

As You Read:

Think about what Koa Halpern is doing to help others.

After You Read:

Use information from the biography to write an opinion essay about Koa Halpern's future.

Lesson Checklist

Check off each task after you complete it.

☐ **Learn Vocabulary**

☐ **Read the Biography:** *Koa Halpern*

☐ **Answer Questions About the Biography**

☐ **Organize Information**

☐ **Write an Opinion Essay**

☐ **Evaluate Your Writing**

Learn Vocabulary

Read the word and its definition.
Then write the vocabulary word on the line.

1. **capital**   money that is used to start a business   _____

2. **ethics**   a set of positive or negative moral beliefs   _____

3. **foreign exchange student**   someone who travels to or from a foreign country for schooling for a limited amount of time   _____

4. **nonprofit**   an organization that does work as a public service, not to earn money   _____

5. **obesity**   the state of being overweight   _____

6. **vegetarian**   a person who does not eat meat, and sometimes no animal products   _____

7. **welfare**   the state of being healthy or doing well; well-being   _____

Koa Halpern

Do you know what it takes to make a quarter pound of beef for just one hamburger? It takes 55 square feet of rainforest land. This is one of the statistics that 15-year-old Koa Halpern likes to share with his audiences. Halpern is the founder of Fast Food Free, a nonprofit organization that educates people of all ages about the problems of eating a fast-food diet. Halpern started Fast Food Free in 2008, when he was just 10 years old.

Koa Halpern

Halpern was raised as a vegetarian, so he had not given much thought to fast food or the problems associated with it. That changed when Halpern's family hosted a foreign exchange student. One of the first things their guest wanted to do was eat at a fast-food restaurant. Halpern wondered what the appeal was. His curiosity led him to study the subject for a school research paper.

Halpern found that, besides being unhealthy, fast food can also hurt the environment. His concerns grew as he learned more about how fast food relates to nutrition and obesity, animal welfare, and the ethics of the farmers who grow the food. He wanted to find positive ways to help, so he looked for a nonprofit organization to join. Until then, there were many causes Halpern had wanted to support, but nothing appealed to him as much as educating people about the dangers of fast food. When he could not find an organization to join, he created his own.

Eventually, Halpern created a website called fastfoodfree.org. Before that, however, he had to raise the capital to fund the site. And as with everything Halpern does, he took on the challenge with passion.

Halpern played his violin at the 16th Street Mall in his hometown of Denver, Colorado, to earn the money he needed. Now it was time for the real work.

The goal of Fast Food Free was to "get people to eat less fast food through education and community awareness, which results in healthier people and a better world." On his website, Halpern provides information about the

To support his cause, Koa Halpern created a website called fastfoodfree.org.

problems associated with fast food and simple steps people can take to change their habits: set a clear goal, plan snacks ahead, create a buddy system, and change your routine.

In the beginning, there seemed to be little interest—until Halpern got a request for an interview with a Denver magazine. That led to an appearance on a national TV network and another article in a major newspaper. Soon, Halpern's calendar was filled with events that would help him spread his message.

Today, Fast Food Free has changed from mainly targeting obesity and environmental issues associated with fast food to broader health concerns. People who visit the website can find out more about the organization and Halpern's efforts to "change the world one bite at a time."

Answer Questions

Read and answer each question.

1. Koa Halpern's organization works to ____.

    Ⓐ help people make healthy food choices

    Ⓑ end the fast-food industry

    Ⓒ raise money to start nonprofits

2. Halpern first became interested in fast food when ____.

    Ⓐ he was interviewed by a Denver magazine

    Ⓑ his teacher assigned the topic for a school project

    Ⓒ his family hosted a foreign exchange student

3. How did Halpern get the money to start his website?

    Ⓐ A nonprofit organization donated it to him.

    Ⓑ He raised money by playing his violin.

    Ⓒ Television viewers sent him money.

4. How old was Halpern when he started fastfoodfree.org?

    Ⓐ 10

    Ⓑ 15

    Ⓒ 16

5. Why might a person from another country want to visit an American fast-food restaurant?

    _____

    _____

6. Would you be interested in joining Halpern's organization? Why or why not?

    _____

    _____

Text-Based Writing: Nonfiction • EMC 6446 • © Evan-Moor Corp.

Organize Information

Read the biography again. Then write information in the graphic organizer that tells your opinion about whether Koa Halpern will or will not make a difference in the world. List facts or reasons that support your opinion.

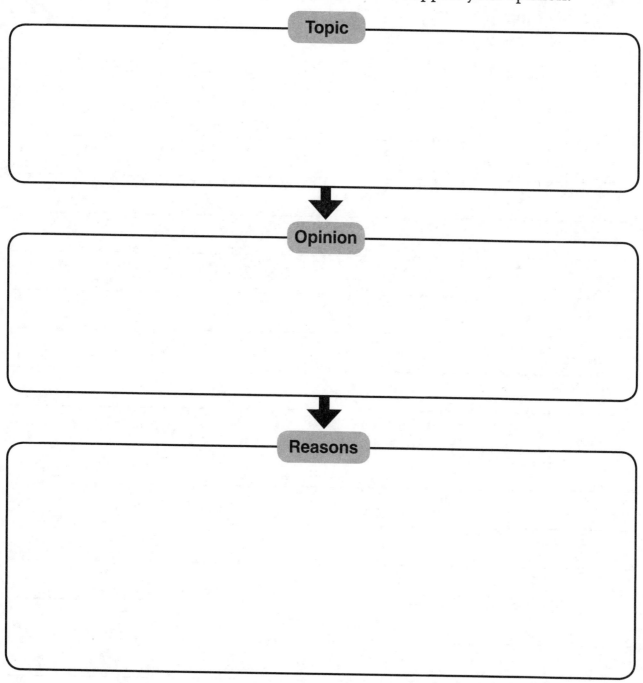

Topic

Opinion

Reasons

Opinion

Write an opinion essay about **Koa Halpern's decision to start a nonprofit organization.** Do you think Koa Halpern will make a difference in the world? Why or why not? Use information from your graphic organizer and the biography.

_____

Title

_____

_____

_____

_____

_____

_____

_____

_____

_____

_____

_____

_____

_____

Evaluate Your Writing

Read about the opinion structure. Then use your essay to complete the activity below.

> A text that gives an **opinion** tells how you personally feel about a subject and why you feel that way. It also includes reasons that support your opinion.

The reason for writing is clear.

My essay explained my opinion and the reasons for my opinion about:

_____

I used these opinion signal words:

_____   _____   _____

I provided reasons that support my opinion.

I included these reasons:

1. _____

2. _____

My last paragraph has a strong conclusion.

My opening sentence for the last paragraph is:

_____

My conclusion sentence for the last paragraph is:

_____

Safety First

Unit Focus

You are going to read a social studies article about unexpected weather events and emergency situations.

As You Read:

Think about why it is important to be prepared for emergencies.

After You Read:

Use information from the article to write an opinion essay about being prepared for various events.

Lesson Checklist

Check off each task after you complete it.

- [ ] **Learn Vocabulary**
- [ ] **Read the Social Studies Article:** *Safety First*
- [ ] **Answer Questions About the Social Studies Article**
- [ ] **Organize Information**
- [ ] **Write an Opinion Essay**
- [ ] **Evaluate Your Writing**

 Text-Based Writing: Nonfiction • EMC 6446 • © Evan-Moor Corp.

Learn Vocabulary

Read the word and its definition.
Then write the vocabulary word on the line.

1. **blizzards**   strong, windy snowstorms that greatly reduce visibility

_____

2. **fault lines**   areas where Earth's tectonic plates meet or rub against each other, resulting in earthquakes

_____

3. **hazards**   dangers or risks

_____

4. **hurricanes**   large, dangerous storms that begin over the ocean

_____

5. **manage**   to take care of and make decisions about

_____

6. **precautions**   positive actions taken in advance of an event or emergency; preparations

_____

7. **predictable**   expected

_____

8. **tornadoes**   strong, swirling windstorms that happen on land

_____

Safety First

Being prepared for events in our lives—no matter how big or small—helps make our lives better. For example, getting a dog is a better experience if you are prepared with information about the breed and have the supplies the dog will need—food, a bed, and toys. Preparing for a test at school or a sports activity can help ensure that you will be successful. These are types of events that are easy to manage. We know when they are going to happen, and we have time to prepare. Some events, however, are not predictable. They can occur without warning and may even affect our safety.

Weather can be unpredictable, and that can cause unexpected events to occur. For that reason, it's important to think about what could happen ahead of time. For example, if the power goes out during a storm, would you know what to do? This is an unexpected event that you might not be able to deal with on your own, especially in the dark. Ideally, your family would have a plan. For example, you and your family members would know to meet in a certain place inside your home. There would be flashlights and batteries in a special drawer you all know about. It's likely that your family does put safety first and has one or more plans in place.

Similarly, every city has a plan for different types of weather events and conditions. During a heavy rainstorm, for example, a tree might fall across a road or there might be flooding. There are city workers who know just what to do in these types of situations. These workers have detailed plans that are designed to help keep people calm and safe. Communities have programs that teach people about these plans so that the people know exactly what to do in case of a weather event.

There are other types of events, or emergencies, that happen in nature that require special planning, preparations, and workers in order to keep people safe. Tornadoes, earthquakes, and hurricanes are a few examples. These types of events tend to occur in certain parts of the country or the world. By learning about what types of events can happen in a particular area, people can take the precautions necessary to help protect themselves. For example, people who live where it snows are likely to prepare themselves for blizzards. People who live in cities and towns located along active fault lines should know all they can about the hazards of earthquakes and the steps to take when one occurs. Knowledge about specific geological or weather hazards in your area is one of the best ways to be prepared.

Some events that can cause dangerous conditions for people do not occur as a result of nature. These events are caused by humans. Some examples are oil spills, chemical leaks, serious flu viruses, and some wildfires. Each type of emergency has its own set of guidelines for response and recovery.

There are many agencies dedicated to keeping people informed and safe no matter what the situation. The Red Cross, the Federal Emergency Management Agency (FEMA), and the Centers for Disease Control and Prevention (CDC) all offer helpful tips on how to get prepared. You can go to their websites for specific information. The chart below lists just a few emergency situations and suggested actions.

NATURAL DISASTERS		
Emergency Situation	**Action Plan**	**Supplies**
Downed Power Line	Call the power company; do not approach the power line.	Create a list of power company telephone numbers for your area.
Tornado	Seek shelter in a basement, a room without windows, or a bathtub.	Create a kit that includes a battery-powered radio, water, and flashlights.
Earthquake	Go outside into a safe open area or take shelter in a doorway or against an inside wall.	Create a kit that includes a battery-powered radio, water, flashlights, and basic supplies you would need for up to three days.
Blizzard	Keep yourself as warm and dry as possible. Stay in one location to keep from getting lost.	Equip the family vehicle's trunk with blankets, matches, candles, and flares.

Answer Questions

Read and answer each question.

1. You need to be prepared for many types of events because ____.

    Ⓐ emergency situations can be unpredictable

    Ⓑ you may need to help fix a downed power line

    Ⓒ blizzards and earthquakes happen often

2. People who live near fault lines need to be most prepared for ____.

    Ⓐ tornadoes

    Ⓑ floods

    Ⓒ earthquakes

3. Which of these events is <u>not</u> considered to be a result of nature?

    Ⓐ a tornado

    Ⓑ an oil spill

    Ⓒ an earthquake

4. Which of the following is recommended during a blizzard?

    Ⓐ going to the basement

    Ⓑ getting a battery-powered radio

    Ⓒ keeping yourself as warm and dry as possible

5. How might people in an area that has tornadoes prepare for a disaster?

    _____

    _____

    _____

6. What type of natural emergency do you need to be most prepared for? Why?

    _____

    _____

Organize Information

Read the social studies article again. Then write information in the graphic organizer that tells your opinion about whether it is or is not important to be prepared for any kind of dangerous conditions or emergency. Include reasons that support your opinion.

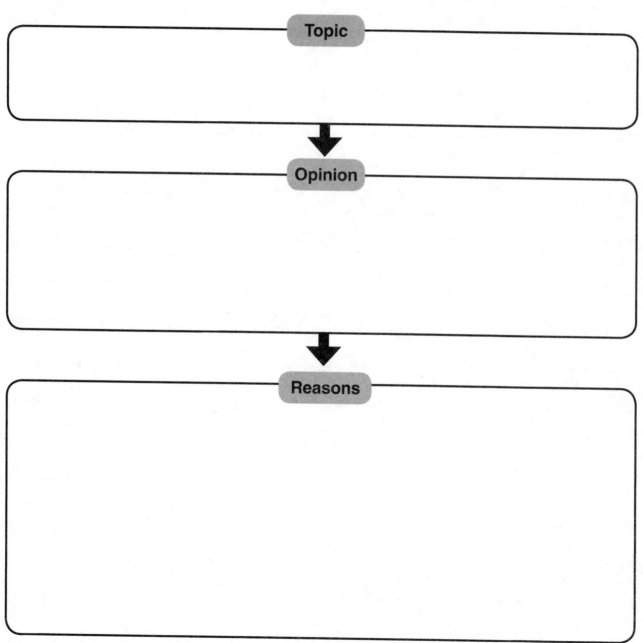

Topic

Opinion

Reasons

Opinion

Write an opinion essay about **whether you do or do not need to be prepared for any kind of dangerous conditions or emergency.** Use information from your graphic organizer and the social studies article.

_____
Title

_____

_____

_____

_____

_____

_____

_____

_____

_____

_____

_____

_____

_____

_____

Evaluate Your Writing

Read about the opinion structure. Then use your essay to complete the activity below.

A text that gives an **opinion** tells how you personally feel about a subject and why you feel that way. It also includes reasons that support your opinion.

The reason for writing is clear.

My essay explained my opinion and the reasons for my opinion about:

_____

I used these opinion signal words:

_____   _____   _____

I provided reasons that support my opinion.

I included these reasons:

1. _____

2. _____

My last paragraph has a strong conclusion.

My opening sentence for the last paragraph is:

_____

My conclusion sentence for the last paragraph is:

_____

Bioengineering

Unit Focus

You are going to read a technology article about bioengineering.

As You Read:

Think about whether bioengineering is or is not useful.

After You Read:

Use information from the article to write an opinion essay about whether we should or should not use bioengineering.

Lesson Checklist

Check off each task after you complete it.

- [ ] **Learn Vocabulary**
- [ ] **Read the Technology Article:** *Bioengineering*
- [ ] **Answer Questions About the Technology Article**
- [ ] **Organize Information**
- [ ] **Write an Opinion Essay**
- [ ] **Evaluate Your Writing**

Learn Vocabulary

Read the word and its definition.
Then write the vocabulary word on the line.

1. **concave**   curved inward like a bowl   _____

2. **efficient**   working in the best or fastest way possible   _____

3. **eliminating**   getting rid of; ending or destroying   _____

4. **nose cone**   a cone-shaped piece of equipment on the front of a machine   _____

5. **rattle**   to make short, rapid knocking sounds, usually by shaking   _____

6. **reputation**   goodness or badness in relation to one's character or business   _____

7. **serrations**   a series of sharp saw-like notches, such as on the blade of a knife   _____

Bioengineering

In Japan, there are high-speed trains, also known as bullet trains, called Shinkansen. These trains move safely at speeds of up to 200 miles per hour. They are currently among the fastest trains in the world. Innovations like the Shinkansen have given Japan a reputation as one of the world's most technologically advanced nations. When the designers of these trains set out to make improvements, they found an unlikely inspiration—a bird.

The kingfisher is a species of bird that is best known for its beak. The long, tapered shape of the beak allows the bird to glide quickly through the air. It also allows the bird to dive deep into the water with a smooth motion and without splashing. This creates an efficient and streamlined way for the bird to fish. What does that have to do with the motion of a train? It's all in the nose—or the nose cone.

The first Shinkansen trains that were produced made extremely loud noises when they passed through tunnels. The change in air pressure as a train moved from inside the tunnel to the outside caused a booming noise. The noise was loud enough to rattle windows, and it could be heard from miles away. The designers were faced with the challenge of eliminating the noise.

When the designers studied kingfishers, they saw a similarity between the way the kingfishers hit the water and how the trains exited

Kingfisher

Shinkansen train

Text-Based Writing: Nonfiction • EMC 6446 • © Evan-Moor Corp.

tunnels—with a lot of pressure. The solution was to mimic something found in nature. This is known as biomimicry, or biologically inspired engineering. The designers made a nose cone for the front car of the train. The nose cone looked like and operated in a similar way to a kingfisher's pointed beak. The improved bullet train was quieter, used less energy, and moved even faster.

Two other engineering problems were solved with the help of biomimicry, as indicated in the chart.

Problem	Animal	Characteristic	Solution
Part of the train vibrated loudly and made an extremely loud noise.	**Barn owl**	Some owls have concave faces that collect sound waves and direct them toward the owls' ears. They also have tiny serrations on their main feathers, which help them move quickly and quietly.	That part of the train was redesigned to look like an owl's wing. Engineers added the tiny serrations, which stopped the vibration and made the train far quieter.
A support frame on the train resisted wind, which created a lot of noise.	**Adélie penguin**	Adélie penguins have bodies that are shaped like footballs. This shape helps them move easily and smoothly through water as they hunt for fish.	The support frame was redesigned to look like the Adélie penguin's body. This helped the train move without creating as much sound.

People do not always make the connection between nature and technology. However, there is much we can learn from our feathered, winged, and finned friends about how to move more efficiently throughout the world.

Answer Questions

Read and answer each question.

1. The nose cones on Shinkansen trains are designed to look like _____.

    Ⓐ owl wings

    Ⓑ kingfisher beaks

    Ⓒ Adélie penguin bodies

2. The process of incorporating a design from nature into technology is known as _____.

    Ⓐ biomimicry

    Ⓑ serration

    Ⓒ innovation

3. Researchers were highly interested in how an Adélie penguin's body _____.

    Ⓐ hit water

    Ⓑ exited water

    Ⓒ moved through water

4. How does an owl's concave face help it?

    Ⓐ It helps the owl fly faster.

    Ⓑ It helps the owl hear sounds better.

    Ⓒ It helps the owl move quickly through water.

5. Why would people who live near Shinkansen trains want them to be quieter?

    _____

    _____

6. Why might some people feel there is little or no connection between nature and technology?

    _____

    _____

Organize Information

Read the technology article again. Then write information in the graphic organizer that tells your opinion about whether it is or is not a good idea to study nature in order to improve technology. List facts or reasons that support your opinion.

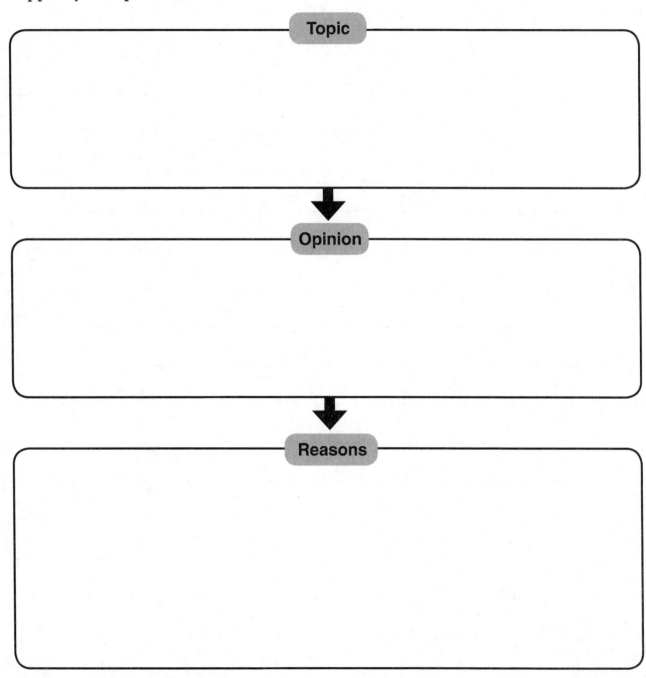

Topic

Opinion

Reasons

Opinion

Write an opinion essay about **whether it is or is not a good idea to study nature in order to improve technology.** Why or why not? Use information from your graphic organizer and the technology article.

_____

Title

_____

_____

_____

_____

_____

_____

_____

_____

_____

_____

_____

_____

_____

_____

Evaluate Your Writing

Read about the opinion structure. Then use your essay to complete the activity below.

> A text that gives an **opinion** tells how you personally feel about a subject and why you feel that way. It also includes reasons that support your opinion.

The reason for writing is clear.

My essay explained my opinion and the reasons for my opinion about:

_____

I used these opinion signal words:

_____   _____   _____

I provided reasons that support my opinion.

I included these reasons:

1. _____

2. _____

My last paragraph has a strong conclusion.

My opening sentence for the last paragraph is:

_____

My conclusion sentence for the last paragraph is:

_____

UNIT
11

A Penny's Worth

Unit Focus

You are going to read a social studies article about the penny.

As You Read:

Think about what the penny means to some people and what it is worth.

After You Read:

Use information from the article to write an argument essay about whether the United States should or should not keep making the penny.

Lesson Checklist

Check off each task after you complete it.

☐ **Learn Vocabulary**

☐ **Read the Social Studies Article:** *A Penny's Worth*

☐ **Answer Questions About the Social Studies Article**

☐ **Organize Information**

☐ **Write an Argument Essay**

☐ **Evaluate Your Writing**

Learn Vocabulary

Read the word and its definition.
Then write the vocabulary word on the line.

1. **assassinated**   intentionally killed   _____

2. **bills**   written laws that have to be
voted upon to be passed   _____

3. **charities**   organizations that raise money
for good causes, such as the
homeless or medical research   _____

4. **circulation**   the movement of items between
people and different places   _____

5. **coating**   a light covering on the outer
surface   _____

6. **contributors**   people who give donations   _____

7. **denomination**   the size, form, or value
of money   _____

8. **nostalgic**   relating fondly to the past or
to history   _____

9. **worth**   having the same value as;
value in money   _____

A Penny's Worth

Some people wonder whether the penny should be made anymore. They say a penny is useless because it can't buy much—not even a piece of chewing gum. But other people want the penny to continue to be made—not because it is worth a lot of money but because it has a lot of meaning.

In 1793, the first coin was made in the United States—the one-cent coin. It was made by the United States Mint, which is the place that strikes, or makes, all of the coins used in this country. The first one-cent coin didn't look like the penny you see today because it didn't have President Lincoln's picture on it. The U.S. Mint started making the Lincoln penny in 1909.

Over the centuries, many different metals such as bronze or tin have been used to make the penny. Different metals were used depending on their value. The first metal used was copper, but when the price of copper went up, pennies were then made of less valuable metals. Today's pennies are made mostly of zinc and have only a thin coating of copper. The metal is not worth very much.

Some argue that the government should stop making pennies altogether because they are worth so little. Pennies actually cost more to make than they are worth—about two cents each! Pennies are often tossed into drawers or saved in jars. Many pennies end up on the ground or are even thrown away. These lost pennies don't go back into circulation, so what is the point of making more? Some people believe that we should not waste taxpayers' money to make pennies because we all need to save as much money as possible.

In 2001 and in 2006, a member of the U.S. House of Representatives tried to get a law passed that would put an end to the penny. He sent two bills to the House, but the bills did not pass. Other countries, however, including Canada, Australia, and New Zealand, have stopped making their version of the penny. The five-cent coin in Canada is now the coin with the lowest value, which means that the price of items may be rounded up by a few cents.

Even though many Americans are still fighting for the end of the U.S. penny, just as many are fighting to keep it. For many people, the penny is a symbol of our 16th president, Abraham Lincoln. Lincoln served as president from 1861 to 1865, when he was assassinated. He served during the Civil War and put an end to slavery by passing the 13th Amendment to the United States Constitution. Although Lincoln is shown on the five-dollar bill as well, the penny for many is a precious, nostalgic symbol of all that Lincoln stood for as well as an important part of our nation's history.

Those people who are fighting for the penny to stay are also concerned about other issues. For example, the people who work to make pennies would lose their jobs. Charities and other organizations may lose donations that rely on loose change from contributors. And many people don't want to see an increase in prices to make up for the lost cents.

So for now, the penny is here to stay. There may come a time in the near future, however, when the five-cent coin becomes America's lowest denomination. Then the penny would be a thing of the past.

A Penny's Worth

Answer Questions

Read and answer each question.

1. The first Lincoln penny was made by the United States Mint in ____.

   (A) 1793

   (B) 1865

   (C) 1909

2. About how much money does it cost the U.S. to make each penny today?

   (A) one cent

   (B) two cents

   (C) five cents

3. Today, pennies are mostly made of ____.

   (A) tin

   (B) copper

   (C) zinc

4. Many people want to keep the penny because ____.

   (A) they do not want prices to be increased

   (B) other countries have stopped using one-cent coins

   (C) it is inexpensive to make pennies

5. Why didn't the first U.S. penny include President Lincoln's image?

   _____

   _____

6. Why might some people throw away pennies even though they are worth money?

   _____

   _____

Text-Based Writing: Nonfiction • EMC 6446 • © Evan-Moor Corp.

Organize Information

Read the social studies article again. Then write information in the graphic organizer that makes an argument for or against keeping the United States penny. Include reasons that support your argument.

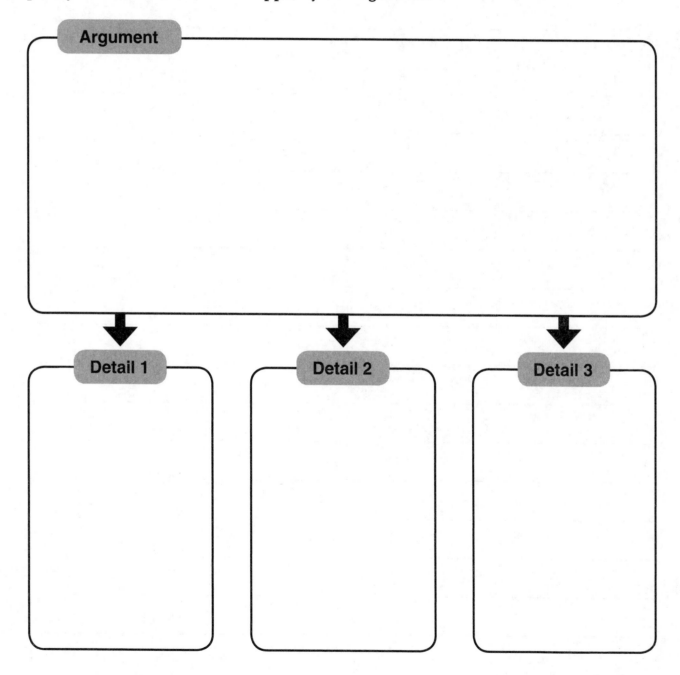

Argument

Detail 1

Detail 2

Detail 3

Argument

Write an argument essay **for or against keeping the United States penny**. Use information from your graphic organizer and the social studies article.

_____

Title

_____

_____

_____

_____

_____

_____

_____

_____

_____

_____

_____

_____

_____

Evaluate Your Writing

Read about the argument structure. Then use your essay to complete the activity below.

> A text that **argues** makes an argument for or against something. It also includes facts or reasons that support the argument.

The reason for writing is clear.

My essay argued that:

_____

I introduced the subject in this topic sentence:

_____

I provided facts or reasons that support my argument.

I included these facts or reasons:

1. _____

2. _____

My paragraphs have a clear focus.

My first paragraph explains that:

_____

My last paragraph includes this conclusion sentence:

_____

UNIT 12

The Science of Flavor

Unit Focus

You are going to read a science article about food flavoring.

As You Read:

Think about what food flavorists do and why.

After You Read:

Use information from the article to write an argument essay for or against artificial food flavoring.

Lesson Checklist

Check off each task after you complete it.

- [ ] **Learn Vocabulary**
- [ ] **Read the Science Article:** *The Science of Flavor*
- [ ] **Answer Questions About the Science Article**
- [ ] **Organize Information**
- [ ] **Write an Argument Essay**
- [ ] **Evaluate Your Writing**

Learn Vocabulary

Read the word and its definition.
Then write the vocabulary word on the line.

1. **artificial**   fake; not real   _____

2. **bureau**   a department or division
of the government   _____

3. **contracts**   written legal agreements that
are signed by two or more
parties   _____

4. **keen**   very good; excellent   _____

5. **manufacturers**   companies that make goods
to sell to businesses or people   _____

6. **preserved**   kept from spoiling or rotting;
saved for future use   _____

7. **processed food**   food that has been modified
to last longer or taste better;
food that is not natural   _____

8. **qualify**   to be able to do something
as a result of schooling or
training   _____

The Science of Flavor

Think of a flavor you like. Maybe you love the taste of bacon. You do not have to fry actual bacon to enjoy this flavor. There are a lot of foods you can buy that are made to taste like bacon—crackers, popcorn, and even ice cream! But how does a taste like bacon get into ice cream?

As strange as it might seem, making flavors for food is a real profession. People who have this job are called flavorists, but they can also be known as food chemists or food research scientists. They work to figure out which flavors people like and

how to best re-create those flavors. Tasting the flavors is a big part of the job, but there is much more to it. While it's true that a flavorist must have a keen sense of taste and smell, a flavorist also usually needs a degree in chemistry or food science to qualify for this position.

Flavorists are hired by large food-and-drink companies to work in their flavor departments. In the lab, flavorists mix chemicals to create both artificial and natural flavors. They try to create new, unique flavors that their competitors don't offer, as well as less expensive versions of flavors that already exist. For example, to make vanilla flavoring using the vanilla bean can be very expensive. A flavorist can copy the taste of vanilla by mixing certain chemicals at a far lower cost. Because of the fierce competition in the food-and-drink industry, businesses are very protective of the flavors they create. In fact, workers in a flavor department often have to sign contracts agreeing to not reveal any of the company's flavor recipes.

Before the early 1900s, most homes in the United States did not have refrigerators. People grew gardens, cared for livestock, or hunted for their food. Some foods could be preserved through drying or canning, but other foods had to be eaten fresh because the food couldn't be preserved without refrigeration. As more people moved to cities, they bought more food from markets. Business owners who sold the food to the markets had to find new and creative ways to keep the food fresh and safe to eat for longer and longer amounts of time. They used chemicals to preserve the food until it was delivered to customers.

Over time, people were able to buy more types of preserved, or processed, food, but the manufacturers found a problem—it did not taste the same as fresh food. Processed food didn't have a lot of flavor, so customers complained and stopped buying certain brands. And manufacturers had another problem—some people did not want artificial flavoring and preservatives added to their foods. They believed that preservatives could be harmful. Also, preserving food meant that food from local farms was being replaced by preserved fruits and vegetables from larger farms that were far away. This made it difficult for local farmers to sell their fresh food. Because the manufacturers were in the business of preserving and flavoring food, not selling fresh food, they had to find a way to make preserved food taste better. Their solution was to use more complex mixtures of chemicals. But this was not something that just anyone could do. Only people with a certain kind of education or set of skills were qualified to do the job. Those people became known as flavorists. Today, almost everything we eat and drink includes the artificial flavors that flavorists make. Depending on how you feel about artifical flavoring, this could be a good thing or a bad thing. Either way, the road to becoming a flavorist isn't easy. After getting a college degree, a person would follow these steps provided by the Bureau of Labor Statistics:

1 Train for five years in a lab.

2 Take and pass a test to become a junior flavorist.

3 After two years, take and pass another test to become an official flavorist.

Answer Questions

Read and answer each question.

1. Which degree would be the best to have if you wanted to be a flavorist?

   Ⓐ statistics

   Ⓑ business

   Ⓒ chemistry

2. Flavorists create new flavors by ____.

   Ⓐ mixing various chemicals

   Ⓑ refrigerating fresh food

   Ⓒ testing flavors at grocery stores

3. What was the main food-related problem for people who lived before the early 1900s?

   Ⓐ natural food that tasted bad

   Ⓑ lack of refrigeration

   Ⓒ unsuccessful gardening

4. How many years would it take to become a flavorist after you've graduated from college?

   Ⓐ 2 years

   Ⓑ 5 years

   Ⓒ 7 years

5. Some people do not approve of artificial flavoring. Why do you think they feel this way?

   _____

   _____

6. How would food be different today if flavorists did not exist?

   _____

   _____

Organize Information

Read the science article again. Then write information in the graphic organizer that makes an argument for or against eating foods that have artificial flavoring. Include reasons that support your argument.

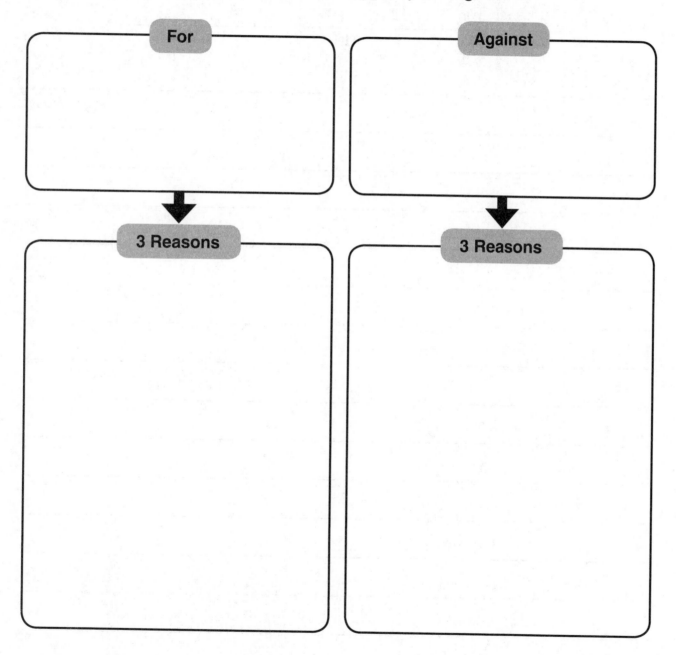

For

Against

3 Reasons

3 Reasons

Argument

Write an argument essay **for or against eating artificially flavored foods.**
Use information from your graphic organizer and the science article.

_____
Title

_____

_____

_____

_____

_____

_____

_____

_____

_____

_____

_____

_____

_____

Evaluate Your Writing

Read about the argument structure. Then use your essay to complete the activity below.

> A text that **argues** makes an argument for or against something. It also includes facts or reasons that support the argument.

The reason for writing is clear.

My essay argued that:

_____

I introduced the subject in this topic sentence:

_____

I provided facts or reasons that support my argument.

I included these facts or reasons:

1. _____

2. _____

My paragraphs have a clear focus.

My first paragraph explains that:

_____

My last paragraph includes this conclusion sentence:

_____

Notes

Notes

Notes

Notes

_____

_____

_____

_____

_____

_____

_____

_____

_____

_____

_____

_____

_____

_____

_____

_____

_____

_____

_____

_____

Notes

Notes

Notes

Notes

_____

_____

_____

_____

_____

_____

_____

_____

_____

_____

_____

_____

_____

_____

_____

_____

_____

Notes

Notes

Notes

Notes

_____

_____

_____

_____

_____

_____

_____

_____

_____

_____

_____

_____

_____

_____

_____

_____

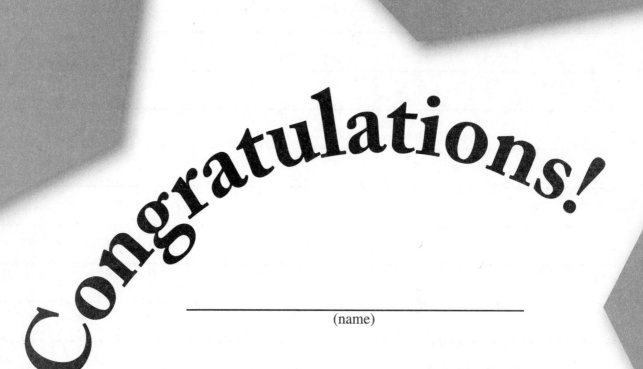

Congratulations!

_____
(name)

You have successfully completed your writing practice!